For Kit

Steve Gilroy

IN THE MIDDLE OF THE WEST

OBERON BOOKS
LONDON

WWW.OBERONBOOKS.COM

First published in 2018 by Oberon Books Ltd
521 Caledonian Road, London N7 9RH
Tel: +44 (0) 20 7607 3637 / Fax: +44 (0) 20 7607 3629
e-mail: info@oberonbooks.com
www.oberonbooks.com

PB ISBN: 9781786826886
E ISBN: 9781786826879

Cover photo by Bryan Cardinale-Powell

Visit www.oberonbooks.com to read more about all our books and to buy them. You
will also find features, author interviews and news of any author events, and you can
sign up for e-newsletters so that you're always first to hear about our new releases.

10 9 8 7 6 5 4 3 2 1

In the Middle of the West was first presented by Oklahoma City University School of Theatre under its original title "The Oklahoma City Bombing Project'. The production was performed in the Burg Theatre and ran April 16th – 19th, 2015. The cast was as follows:

CHRIS SHOLER / STEPHEN JONES	Tanner Bradshaw
RON NORICK / ANDREW ROY / BUD WELCH	Cody Wimmer
CLAUDE THOMAS / CHRIS FIELDS	Ian McGee
SAM GONZALES / MARK BAYS	Ben Roberts
GARY MARRS / IMAD ENCHASSI / INSTRUMENTALIST / SERVER	JD Whigham
JANET BECK / REBECCA DENNY	Amy Fuhrman
JAN HENRY / SUSAN WINCHESTER / POLLY NICHOLS	Emily Hawkins
JANE THOMAS / CHRISTI YOUNG / SINGER	Lauren Lynn Matheny
CLAIRE BOLDERSON / BELLA KOK / CHRISTY SMITH	Elizabeth McCreight
WAITRESS / AREN ALMON-KOK	Corrinne Mica
JENIFER REYNOLDS / FLORENCE ROGERS	Michelle Roselle

Creative Team

Director	Courtney DiBello
Scenic/Projections Designer	Jason Foreman
Costume Designer	Chloe Chafetz
Lighting Designer	Travis Baldwin
Sound Designer	LukE Hadsall
Dramaturg	H. Brooke Hessler
Stage Manager	Bryan Bauer
Commissioning Producer	Brian D. Parsons
Artistic Director of TheatreOCU	D. Lance Marsh
Dean of the School of Theatre	Mark Edward Parker
Associate Dean of the School of Theatre	Brian D. Parsons

The UK premiere of **In the Middle of the West** was performed at Northern Stage, Newcastle upon Tyne from the 18th – 21st May 2016. The original cast were; Lauren Batey, Rebecca Betts, Paula Clayton, Russell Edge, Ashley Fraser, Matthew Geddis, Rachael Harvey, Jenna Hayward, Carl McKay, Victoria McLaughlin, Ellie McPhail, Amy Monaghan, Tiwai Musa, Andrew Rakowski, Krystina Robinson, Fleur Rozen, Olivia Taylor, Christopher Walton, Aman Virmani.

Director	Steve Gilroy
Lighting Design	Kev Tweedy
Sound Design/Music Direction	Jeremy Bradfield
Stage Manager	Nichola Reilly

SPECIAL THANKS

A special thank you to all those interviewed as part of the creation of this play. Whether your story is directly told or not, you are part of the fabric of Oklahoma City's recovery and regeneration.

Deepest thanks to Kari Watkins at the Oklahoma City National Memorial and Museum for her tireless support of this project. Without her assistance, we would not be able to present such an extraordinary tribute to the people whose stories of resilience and hope are shared in this play.

Brian Parsons, Associate Dean of the School of Theatre

September 2018, Oklahoma City

Steve Gilroy would like to thank

All the transcribers, contributors to the project who generously shared their stories. A special thanks to Jenifer Reynolds for her support and additional testimony for the UK production, the crew of the UK production of **In the Middle of the West**, everyone at Oklahoma City University School of Theatre, Northumbria University – Newcastle, Brooke Hessler, Kate Craddock, Gez Casey, Richard Stockwell.

Oklahoma City University School of Theatre

The School of Theatre at Oklahoma City University offers three pre-professional degrees: BFA Acting; BFA Design and Production, and BA Theatre and Performance. OCU School of Theatre prepares young theatre artists for a sustainable, professional life. The faculty inspire students in a rigorous, disciplined, and collaborative academic and production environment.

The school produces, and co-produces, over 55 productions a year, and acting students' performance work is showcased in Los Angeles, New York, Dallas and Chicago. BFA Design and Production students annually present their work at USITT and KCATF. BA Theatre and Performance students regularly create and present work at Oklahoma Contemporary, Oklahoma City Museum of Art and beyond. The school currently has three professional partners who provide interning and professional opportunities – Lyric Theatre of Oklahoma, Oklahoma City Ballet, and Oklahoma Children's Theatre.

In June 2019 the school will offer a Summer Shakespeare intensive in Washington D.C. in partnership with the Folger Theater, and have plans to launch a new MFA in Screen Acting in 2020, to be taught in Los Angeles and London.

Characters

Characters in order of appearance:

ACT I
                                        Jenifer Reynolds

Sam Gonzales

Waitress

Gary Marrs

Ron Norick

Jan Henry

Chris Sholer

Janet Beck

Jane Thomas

Claude Thomas

Andrew Roy

Claire Bolderson

Imad Enchassi

Aren Almon-Kok

Chris Fields

Bella Kok

ACT II
                                          Mark Bays

Timothy McVeigh

Bud Welch

Stephen Jones

Rebecca Denny

Christy Smith

Bill Clinton

Donald Trump

Florence Rogers

Server

Polly Nichols

The play is largely constructed from interviews conducted in Oklahoma City, USA, London, England and Newcastle upon Tyne during 2015 and 2016.

Notes:

When performing it's useful to consider the nature of "everyday" speech. The ellipses, the patterns, the "ums" and "uhs" and the pace. In general conversation people often speak much quicker than one would imagine so it's important where appropriate to play the text with pace and energy.

Words in square brackets [ ] are not spoken, but are for clarification of meaning.

A stroke (/) indicates the point of interruption by the following speaker or character. A character's line placed within the text of another indicates that the latter continues uninterrupted. For example:

> CLAIRE: I think you got there sooner. *(ANDREW: Yeah.)* I got there the next day. *(ANDREW: I got–)* And you had a lot of delays, getting there, it was trouble it was really difficult I remember, I think you called from the plane or something?

"slides" refer to the projection of the text described. This could be a conventional projection onto a screen or a wall, or it could just be cardboard signs. The point in most cases is to identify the person/s. Not all projected slides are referred to in the text, but assume there is one per character. The slides should dissolve in. And then out.

In the original production a minimal set comprised a number of chairs which is equal to the number of actors in the cast. The chairs are wooden, old, and a little battered. They are not of uniform design.

In the original production most of the songs were accompanied by a simple guitar but included vocal harmony arrangements.

The play was originally performed with 11 performers in Oklahoma City and 17 performers in the UK. For smaller casts, performers can play multiple parts.

The characters Timothy McVeigh and Donald Trump were not represented in the original Oklahoma City University production.

SCENE 1

Blackout.

Lights up. The stage is bathed in warm light, some birds are singing. The Company are onstage.

CHARACTER A: Something about a bright early morning in Oklahoma / City.

CHARACTER B: The sky is *so* clear.

CHARACTER A: Yes. So blue, quite an intense ...

CHARACTER B: The air is still.

   Beat.

CHARACTER A: This isn't typical.

CHARACTER B: *(Agrees.)* No.

CHARACTER A: Not for / April.

CHARACTER B: Not for / April.

CHARACTER A: *(Agrees.)* No. *(Short pause.)* It's a vibrant sky.

CHARACTER B: But still.

CHARACTER A: Unusual.

CHARACTER B: Oklahoma skies are always busy ...

CHARACTER A: Weather here is *always* busy.

CHARACTER A: Such a pretty / morning.

CHARACTER A: Just after Easter.

CHARACTER A: So still.

CHARACTER A: Blue.

   Pause.

SCENE 2

The loud "clunk" of a large power switch to "off". The stage changes to cold steel. The Company look out to the audience. Pause. All are still and then together, the cast take a sharp intake of breath – a gasp – for air. Beat.

The loud sounds of the bombing aftermath; sirens, helicopters, etc. What follows are the edited actual words spoken by witnesses of the bombing from the documentary "Terror Hits Home" 1995. Vocally the actors replicate the voices of their characters, but with volume and energy. Some use megaphones. The stage is transformed into the chaotic aftermath of a bombing. A physically frenetic scene. The actors randomly echo/repeat each other's lines and this becomes more pronounced with repeated echoed voices.

CHARACTER 1: The side of the federal Building has been blown / off

CHARACTER 2: A tremendous blast came in through the windows, blew us out of our chairs and onto the / floors.

CHARACTER 3: I thank the Lord that I wasn't sitting at my desk at that time, because that portion of the building, that portion of the building has / gone.

CHARACTER 4: They are bringing people out who that just covered in blood ehm, ambulance crews have been arriving for the last ten minutes and they're going into / the building.

CHARACTER 5: We've got a lot of children hurt over here at the / YMCA!

CHARACTER 6: The devastation at the Alfred P Murrah building appears to be / almost uh, total.

CHARACTER 7: I don't know what happened, just a / blast.

CHARACTER 8: I was falling and then I hit and I was dazed for a minute and I realized it had to be an / explosion or something.

CHARACTER 9: The large church at the corner of fourth and Harvey all the stained glass windows have been blown out … it is chaos / down here.

CHARACTER 10: At the federal building there's a children's centre … we need to get some fire officials / up there as soon as possible

At the Creche.

CHARACTER 11: *(To a little girl.)* Can you tell me your name? Can you tell me / your name?

CHARACTER 12: Is there someone there?

AREN: My daughter's one and she's in there.

CHARACTER 13: You went to the / nursery?

CHARACTER 7: Well we were pullin'. We've pulled five little kids out and a couple of / ladies

CHARACTER 14: All we can do is just be of as much assistance as we can to those who are injured and try to get them some medical / care.

CHARACTER 6: You're doing a great job. We, all of us, in Oklahoma City thank you for what you've done today … The devastation in downtown Oklahoma City,/ it's incredible.

CHARACTER 15: Let's / move out!!

The stage starts to empty.

JENIFER: Right be careful, let's just warn them now Cynthia that this is raw tape that we shot at the hospital which we have not censored in any way and you may see some graphic / stuff.

CHARACTER 17: It's just astonishing to me that er an evil human being would do this to children and other innocent people, especially here in the Middle of mid / America.

CHARACTER 6: This is something that happens somewhere else, this is something that happens in places like ... Beirut. Places far, far away with strange sounding names. It's not something that's supposed to happen in places like Oklahoma City. It's not something that's supposed to happen *(Beat.)* at home.

SCENE 3

A member of the Company sings, "By the Time I get to Phoenix" by Glenn Campbell which eventually cross-fades to the recording by Glen Campbell playing on the jukebox of a typical diner.

A diner.

Lights fade up. SAM GONZALES sits in a booth facing the audience with a cup of coffee. A voice recorder sits on the table and opposite SAM. His interviewer is not on stage but signified by an empty chair. She is a young woman. Music fades down. SAM addresses the interviewer.

SAM: We had a Mayor's Prayer Breakfast at the Convention center. We had about twelve hundred people there, big event. *(Slide: Sam Gonzales, seventy-nine years – former Chief of Police.)* uhh I sat at the table with the Fire Chief and the City Manager. *(Referring to diary.)* Started about ... ya know? *Nobody's* seen this ... nobody's read it but me. I kept a diary during the bombing every day. So I can tell you exactly ... the time I left. I think at 8:45 ...

WAITRESS refills SAM's coffee.

SAM: Thanks

WAITRESS: *(Friendly.)* You're very welcome. *(Exits.)*

GARY enters other side of the stage. He never acknowledges the other characters. He addresses the audience directly.

GARY: After the Breakfast we were heading back in my car, *(Slide: Gary Marrs-former Fire Chief.)* headed back to city hall and the explosion occurred while *(Enter RON who also doesn't acknowledge the other characters but addresses the audience directly.)* we were in the car downtown and of course I immediately drove over to the / scene.

RON enters and also does not acknowledge the other characters and addresses the audience directly.

RON: So I had gone to my business office which is uh just South of Baptist Hospital. *(Slide: Ron Norick, former Mayor.)* A five-story building and that building just shook like an earthquake.

SAM: Well, I like most people, when I got there I didn't think it was a bombing. As I approached it, I thought it was gonna be some kind of natural gas explosion … And when I drove up to the scene and saw the / crater …

GARY: Uhm, Gonzalez the police chief told me that he thought he recognized the crater / in front of the building …

SAM: Huge crater out front, of the street, then being a police officer, I knew what it was. It was a car bomb, a truck bomb, some kind of bomb.

RON: It was still smoking y'know, lotta smoke and all that and they said it was a bomb and "What, what d'y'mean a bomb?" … why I'm thinkin' it's either airplanes crashed, gas lines blown up, or fuel truck something like that but not a-not a / bomb.

SAM: You know the first, first couple of hours are chaos. I, I, I, don't care whether it's here, or New York City. *(Pause.)*

There were still a lot of bodies … laying out in open view. Uh, there was a lot of people in the building screaming for help and there was a lot of people, just, just people, not trained people, just / people.

WAITRESS: Not to bother you again Chief, it was in *April* of 1995?

SAM: It was.

WAITRESS: What day?

SAM: Nineteenth.

WAITRESS: *(With pace.)* Well that's what I thought, I was just saying to Jenny it was the 19th, well she's too young to remember anyways, but I told her "You *know* who that is? Well that's Sam Gonalez, 'Oklahoma City Chief of Police', that man's a hero" *(SAM: Oh no …)* *(To the girl interviewer.)* Sorry for interrupting your meeting darlin'. *(WAITRESS goes to leave and then turns.)* Well I might leave you alone now … but I might not, okay?

SAM: *(Laughing.)* That's alright, I don't mind at all. *(WAITRESS exits.)*

RON: It was eh, it was traumatic, because we lost One hundred and sixty-eight people nineteen kids and it took … It was three weeks before we recovered the last two bodies and I was with the families when we recovered the last two

SAM: Oh, I connected with my granddaughter. She was born on March third. My therapy at night was to go home and hug her. I'd rock her in an old rocking chair. That's, probably what I remember most about what uhh helped me make it through … because … we lost a lot of babies … in Oklahoma City … yeah. *(In answer to; "What's her name?")* My granddaughter's name is Harley.

GARY: Yeah well everyone knows about that photo of the baby girl and the firefighter. Yeah, there was somebody in the rubble digging and they pulled that child out and just handed it to Chris, the fire fighter that's in the photo, and wherever that photographer was, he snapped it when Chris had it, so there was a … You see, it wasn't just Chris that had gone in there and rescued the little child, but that photo made it *look* like Chris saved the baby. He tried real hard to make sure everybody understood what happened, that he was no hero. But, as you can imagine uhm when the baby didn't make it and they have the photo of your dead child on Time Magazine and all over the media … it was a very stressful … for the mother. *And* Chris. There was a long time that he would not do interviews or talk about it at all. Chris and the mother; they stayed very close though. In fact, I would imagine they were still close today.

SAM: You know, the, the response in Oklahoma City was different to anywhere else in the United States … when the, New York uhh bombing occurred at the Trade, not the, at the *first* Trade Center bombing in 1993. They had street vendors selling coffee for two dollars to the rescuers. In Oklahoma City coffee was free. The money was called the Oklahoma dollar because if those emergency workers went in a restaurant? They would not have paid for a thing. So they called it an Oklahoma dollar because it could never be spent.

RON: McVeigh thought that by him bombing this federal building on the anniversary of Waco which was two years earlier that … that people would rally around him and overthrow the government. Well, the opposite happened. If this country is attacked, one thing about our citizens we may be democrats or republicans an' we fight but it's kinda like y'know a family. The family will fight, but you better not get in the middle of a family fight … And we're a family and people bonded together …

SAM: We had no looting, uh no looting at all, uh the bank had the windows blown out, was left open for a couple of days. None of the money was missing, all of it was recovered, uh we just didn't / have any looting … so …

GARY: Serving this community has been my life. This is a great city and the citizens are really unique.

SAM: For years; I *talked* about the bombing every day, *thought* about it every day … constantly reliving uhhh, some of the bad stuff. You want to make sure that it … you don't want it to completely define who you are. But sometimes … sometimes that's hard.

RON: I loved being Mayor. I was in office three terms … but I finally just wore out, you just get finally, just, "I'm tired you know, I'm just tired." I got to that point.

RON and GARY look at each other as the lights fade on them both.

SAM: Well, I think you have to separate who you are with what you did. The police chief in Oklahoma City, whoever he would have been, would have done the same things I did. So I needed, to separate, any of the kudos from the job; "Oh look at *me*, I was a police chief, I did *this*, I did *that*", uhh, to not let it, define who I am … or who I was, if that makes sense. *(Pause.)* So this is a theatre project? Are you a theatrical student? *(Listens to answer with interest. He's fond of the girl interviewer.)* My granddaughter, Harley, uhh is in the theatre *(Short pause, WAITRESS passes table.)* I'm gonna order something in just a minute.

WAITRESS: You take your time Chief! You take your time! I'm letting y'all just do y'alls thing and then / I'll …

SAM: Alright.

WAITRESS: You tell me and I'll be here whenever you're ready, you just holler and I'll be right here? Okay? / That's no probem at all.

SAM: Alright. Thank you.

WAITRESS: *(To girl interviewer.)* You've got a beautiful smile sweetheart.

WAITRESS exits. Pause, as SAM sees something familiar in the face of his interviewer,

SAM: Harley, my grandaughter; She's uh … nineteen now, will be twenty in March.

As lights fade on SAM. Four of the Company sing, "Get Down on Your Knees and Pray". The following underscores JENNIFER's speech.

Oh my brother, can't you hear me say
Oh my brother, you'd better get down on your knees and pray
Get down, get down, get down, get down
Get down on your knees and pray

Oh sister, can't you hear me say
Oh sister, you'd better get down on your knees and pray
Get down, get down, get down, get down
Get down on your knees and pray

JENIFER: *(Addressed to the audience through a microphone.)* Okay, well, I mean this has always been the Bible Belt. *(Slide: Jenifer Reynolds, News Anchor, KWTV.)* In this part of the country? We're Baptist and um and that's … there's just a certain mind-set that goes with that. You know, you get blessed in this life because you work hard and um God helps those who help themselves and there's a lot about this … that's really good. I mean, Oklahomans, for example. People who came here were just amazed, we didn't really ever ask for any help. We never looked up and said, "Hey, who's gonna come fix this for us?"

Oklahomans are just … we are self-reliant. And *so* we do not like a government that encourages people to lose that. *And* we're very law and order conscious. If law and order broke down in this city? *(Beat.)* Everybody would go out and re-establish it. That'd be the first thing that would happen. That would be the very first thing.

SCENE 4

CHRIS and JAN stand on either side of the stage. They address the audience directly

CHRIS: I was … actually … taking off the rest of the week and I was driving out to Albuquerque to visit my dad … I was kind of getting up, getting ready to go, *(Slide: Chris Sholer.)* and I had to take the dog to the vet. So I take the dog to the vet … and all the sudden we hear this WOOM. And I'm not … I'm at 122nd and May.

JAN: I was just pulling into Health Science Center. Do you know where that is? Relatively speaking, it's very close. *(Slide: Jan Henry.)* And I was just pulling in to the parking lot and I had my back to the city when the bomb went off. And I didn't know what it was, but it was a / huge explosion.

CHRIS: It sounded like a sonic boom kinda thing and I heard they had some boiler thing go off downtown and I thought, "Oh, okay. No big deal." So, I turned around, and I go home / and I'm packing.

JAN: I turned around and looked and there was this massive plume of white smoke coming up into the sky … I saw, it was downtown. I immediately thought someone had bombed the Courthouse. I was terrified that it was the courthouse and that our clerks … they are like family … I mean, we are so close to these young people.

CHRIS: And I flip the TV on … And immediately saw, you know, the helicopter flying over and the building and I just went, "Oh my god." You know?

And then they were calling for medical personnel to come down to … and I just looked at Jeanie and said, "What do I do?" I said, "I can't leave now." So I called my nurse and said, "I'm picking you up, we're going down to St. Anthony's." And so by the time we got down there, the first wave had kinda come through.

JAN: It wasn't the Courthouse, it was next door. The Murrah Building is immediately across the street, but we all joined and had lunch together. Just kind of to hold to each other. We were so shaken by this, it was unbelievably huge. You just cannot imagine. For a city like this, the magnitude of this event.

CHRIS: They'd gotten the OR's cleared, and so we set up a triage system, and we were, … you know, triaging people that were coming in … you know. But what amazed me, was how quickly without any practice or anything, it got organized. We had, the ERs, you know, manned, with people in every room, you know, so when people came in there was somebody already there.

JAN: You just needed to do something. "Let's go find someplace to donate blood." But there was an enormous line. Six, seven hours long. And we were in line with, ehhm? Three-piece suits and Hells Angels motorcyclists. The array of humanity that was in this building all with the same purpose was *(Beat.)* stunning.

CHRIS: So … you know, we put in a couple of lines, central lines in people, things like that. Hell, I could do that in my sleep. So … but once that first kinda wave hit, and all that, then we just … we were waiting. And we waited. And that was just … that was tough. That was the toughest part. *(Pause.)* They were all gone. I mean by that, by that afternoon, we realised … there were no more coming.

CHRIS sits.

JAN: I'm a dentist. And I was teaching at the dental school at the time. And one of my colleague professors was taking names of everybody that wanted to go down and help. I said, "Put my name on this too." I had never done body identification. I had no experience whatsoever. But, my professor was the chief dental officer and he just trained everybody as we went. And we would take X-rays on the bodies brought in. I mean, dental X-rays on the bodies that were brought in. If we were lucky, we already had dental records there and we could start comparing dental records, which is a really, really good way to identify a body, almost as good a fingerprint.

What did bother me pretty quickly was … everybody had the same expression on their faces. I actually talked to my professor about it because it disturbed me. They looked like, the faces looked like Munch's 'The Scream'. Were they screaming? It was like this; *(Demonstrates the scream with her mouth open.)* He said, "No, no, no. What happens in a bomb, you get this huge blast and your lungs go – *(Gasps in rapidly.)* And that was the expression; they're frozen in their last expression. I just hated the thought that their last moment was of that kind of terror and he said, "They never knew what happened. They never … it was so rapid."

My biggest fear was a child being brought in. You saw the photograph of Baylee, the famous photograph of the firefighter with the baby in his arms? I didn't know how I would handle finding a child.

CHRIS: Hm. Well. The Country itself was looking at us, sort of how we handled this, and the fact that we all came together, everybody jumped in. And my first thought was, that doesn't surprise me at all. That's who we are here. I mean, it's / Oklahoma.

JAN: Here in Oklahoma … "We need more gloves." Truckloads, truckloads would come and same thing with bottled water, food. Everybody was, you know, trying to bring a casserole. This is what we do when there is a disaster of any kind – personal or on a big scale. You've gotta *cook* something and bring it and help.

CHRIS: President Clinton came … and I remember hearing, you know, Clinton talk. It was amazing. You know, regardless of his politics, you know?

JAN: And like I said in the first place, I still hold it as the most positive, best experience I've ever had in my life. It wasn't horrific at all. It was just, it felt so important. *So* important. I've always cherished, cherished the experience.

A B/W film of the 1889 Oklahoma Land Rush projects onto the perimeter fence surrounding the bombed Murrah Building in Oklahoma City. It is accompanied by the sound of school children reenacting the event.

SCENE 5

The Archive. The archive sits beneath the Oklahoma City National Memorial and Museum. JANET tends to some of the items/boxes. The characters are aware of each other and talk directly to the audience speaking to individual members.

JANET: *(To the audience as though they are the children.)* I say to the children *(Firmly.)* "Look at the *facts*, look at what happened that day" I usually will tell them … "It was a *horrific* day."

I'm a volunteer here at the memorial. So this is the erm the archive. *(Slide: Janet.)* Every kind of artifact that you could think of related to the bombing, anything that you can imagine, it's probably here. There's many items that have been collected from the fence; there's combs, Mardi Gras beads, / tassels, flags …

JANE: I never anticipated the fence, nobody dreamed of the fence that took us all by / surprise.

JANET: T-shirts, bears, watches, pacifiers, Oh my God you name it. From '95 till now, we're still collecting them; bringing / them in.

JANE: I had worked with the Oklahoma historical society. I got a letter asking if I'd serve on one of the committees.

JANET: They started the whole thing in the first year and there were these big groups that met. But then once we got that mission statement set that / basically guided everything …

JANE: The whole point was it was a group of people who understood that we needed to think about preserving the materials related to the bombing … and we began to finally start to collect the / materials …

JANET: "That we come here to remember those who died those who survived and those who will be changed forever, may those who leave here know the meaning of violence" … uh I don't remember / all of it.

JANE: So I was driving Claude's car *(To CLAUDE.)* And I was gathering, I was loading all this in the Lincoln; *(Slide: Jane and Claude.)* I couldn't believe all the stuff I could put in that car that you wouldn't put in a car, *(They are both amused by their recollections.)* Oh not just *boxes*, but pieces of *fence*, an elevator *door* … I was putting *(CLAUDE: Yes, in my Lincoln I might add.)* *(She laughs.)* I know! Oh those leather seats! I worried *so* about them, you know? I mean I would … I moved the body bags in it … All kinds of st[uff] … no no no no *(CLAUDE: not the <u>bodies</u>, just the body bags.)* And washtubs and stuff, and this guy said to me one time, "Are you going to haul all these things around in that Lincoln?", and I said "It's all I have!", so Claude comes up and he says you have to have a truck. And that's when you got me that Ford truck.

CLAUDE: Yeah I got /you the little Ford Ranger.

JANE: A Ford / Ranger.

CLAUDE: And she moved stuff for I don't know how many / years.

JANE: I moved unbelievable stuff in that Ford Ranger. My first task was to clean up what I could and sort all the stuff they took out of the building. Now these are people's pictures, the stuff from their desks … I cleaned to the best of my ability and laid them out on a pallet … It was very emotionally taxing … working with the family members and survivors … I put all the pictures together and things and that's when *(Short pause.)* Doris Jones saw the picture of her daughter's … her daughter Carrie Ann died erm in the bombing … it was an ultrasound, of her grandbaby. Her Carrie Ann was pregnant and she had just gotten her ultrasound that morning and Doris was going through it and found her daughter's ultrasound. *(CLAUDE: Yeah.)* And after that. What was left went to the archives.

Pause.

Oh! This is the most important character of all. *(Presents a small teddy bear.)* This is Murray, and he was one of the very first items that I took off of the fence. He's remained my mascot, traveled in several states and had his picture once – in *The New York Times.* And each time, we used to always say that his face started out straight, and each time his nose got a little higher and a little higher over to the side until he got to be a really snooty *(pronounced: "sn-ir-ty".)* bear.

The fence originally went around a large, large area … it was to protect everybody from the site. So, people came and they brought initial like flowers and things … but more and more started coming to the site and tying more and more stuff to the fence. They began to bury it with flowers and um children toys and flags, a lot of flags.

JANET: One of the toughest things that they had to do in the committees, was to define who a survivor was …

JANE: *(Agrees.)* Mmhmmm …

JANET: "Where were you that day?" And if you were on the south side of this street you were not a survivor, if you were on the north side of that street you were. They had to draw a perimeter … people who were a mile away were … "I heard the blast; I'm a survivor", "No you're not." And that was basically to get the names for the Survivor Wall …

JANE: The fence had to be moved permanently and they wanted the survivors, the family members, the rescue workers to be able to move / it …

JANET: We knew it had to be done to build the memorial, there's no way we could build the memorial with a fence right in the middle of it. Initially, the whole big thing was, we want the building to be standing like it is, we want it fenced off we don't want anything done with it, we want people to see it and remember what happened. *(Beat.)* I've been here several times to bring groups of children down and I say *(As if talking to the children.)* "Look at the facts, look at what happened that day" I usually will tell them … "It was a horrific day."

Pause.

If the lights went out in this room now? I'd be under the table. I travelled with a flashlight in my purse for years.

Short pause as JANET recalls the events of that day.

It was pitch dark. It was, it was so dark … we were on the first floor so that everything was coming down on top of us. Our office had very low turnover; most of us had been there twenty plus years. When I got out, one of the younger girls … they got her out and she had asthma and was having a hard time breathing, I stopped to ask if she was okay and she begged me not to leave her … she was scared. And where am I gonna go anyway? I didn't know what was going on … at least I could help somebody. They brought one of the girls from our office and laid her on the sidewalk and said "Do you know who that is?" And I said "I have no idea', I couldn't recognize her. It was one of our co-workers. They found one of our supervisors who had died and they put her over in a corner so that nobody could walk on her or step on her or anything. It was chaos. It's hard … it's hard … we were like a family, you know?

JANE: *(Holding MURRAY.)* I had a desk; and I plopped him down on my desk … forever more. He became my symbol of hope, of love and understanding … and on the days when it was particularly hard he got me through it.

I read a letter from a child and I may cry telling you this. Isn't that funny this is twenty years and my heart still breaks. I opened a package of letters from a school in Michigan, now think about Terry Nichols, the other bomber he was from Michigan, and this child wrote "Dear children in Oklahoma City, we are not all bad." *(Beat.)* Oh my god. An elementary school child. My heart just broke. Murray got me through that one. We talked about that one.

I was reading the story of the Michigan first responder who wanted to do something in relationship to OKC and they gathered up a bunch of money and they were caravanning a group of first responders to Oklahoma City. They had quite a cash for Oklahoma City and as they got close to the Oklahoma border, they grew concerned about how they would be perceived because they were coming in from Michigan. And when they got close, I'm gonna cry, when they got into the border. They heard over the airways, "This is the highway patrol for Oklahoma and we've come to escort you in … " I'm sorry. That was just so beautiful. They were just so worried about how they were going to be perceived and they were received with open arms.

JANET: *(To the children/audience.)* "Look at the *facts*, see what happened that day … stop and look, see what happened." And then at the end I say … "Bad things may … *are* going to happen … but if something bad happens to you? There's still hope you can still have a future."

JANE: Exactly, exactly. You are on your knees and how do you get the first step up and get back on your feet? For the survivors, it was that old tree leafing out. For family members it was all those messages left on the fence. It's these symbols of hope that just let you, *help you*, put yourself back together. A little bit.

SCENE 6

CHRISTI: We were a very, very, very close family. We are Southern Baptist, and every summer my sister and I went to church camp. In the beginning she loved me because I was her baby sister; but as we grew up I was the bratty *annoying* sister but, she was very protective.

Pam was beautiful, she had beautiful blue eyes, and very striking features. When she walked into a room … she kind of captivated; everyone kind of gravitated toward her.

She loved to go to gay bars and party because she loved to dance. She said the gay men made her feel really good because they would always compliment her.

Tommy was very soft spoken and he loved her because she was very outgoing and they got along so well and became inseparable friends. And he was a hairdresser, had his own business, a very successful business.

Tommy ended up getting HIV. Medicine for anyone who had AIDs back then [in the Eighties] was extremely expensive, and he couldn't afford the insurance. Pam went to my parents and she said "Here's the deal. Tommy has AIDS and he needs insurance and I have great insurance because I work at the hospital and I'd like to marry him so he can be covered by the insurance." My parents said "Well if that's what you think you need to do for him, then you have our blessing."

She married Tommy in '89 and she took very good care of him; it was very hard for her you know he got very, very sick. A lot of her friends died with AIDS and she went to a lot of funerals, she had a lot of sadness. There was … there was conflict with my father. The Bible, you know, was against homosexuality, and I think for that reason he did keep it to himself because of a fear of what the other people of the church would think. But, he would become very defensive when people would say that God gave them AIDS because of *this* sin.

She had called me and said "I don't think he is gonna last much longer, can you come in?" I flew into Oklahoma City and my mom was there. *(Short pause.)* Tommy died that day; and … we were all with him. He was in so much pain and it was such a horrible disease to die from. He was ready.

She was lonely so I flew down to Oklahoma City the next month and we hung out and ate. Ordered pizza and laughed a lot. She was dating someone at the time that she adored, and she was really looking forward to moving into the next stage of her life. Anyway, Social Security had called her and said "We have a cheque for you." She needed to pick it up for Tommy towards funeral expenses and she asked if they could mail it and they said "No you have to come pick it up because we have to see your I.D.." She got there, we think, about three minutes to nine and she was walking into the building, the Murrah Building, when the bomb went off. *(Beat.)* She was found right outside the building.

She nursed Tommy for three years and it wasn't fair to me that she had lost her life when she was just starting to live again.

I felt bad for my parents who had a lot of hatred. You know for McVeigh? I think they finally came to terms with it through prayer.

When I had my first son it was about a year and a half after Pam was killed. We were on the bed and he was laid between my parents and my dad crying and smiling and he said "I didn't think I would ever smile again, I didn't think I would ever laugh again." So we called my son "Our saviour." You know?

SCENE 7

Sound of a helicopter passing overhead. JENIFER sits on the edge of a desk stage right and CLAIRE and ANDREW stand stage left. JENIFER does not acknowledge CLAIRE and ANDREW and they do not acknowledge her. IMAD sits upstage centre left.

JENIFER: Well I was um, I was at KWTV, *(Slide: Jenifer Reynolds.)* was the six and ten anchor at that time … and my … my relationship with it, is that it was … the biggest story, obviously, of, of my career in television.

CLAIRE: We worked in the same / office.

ANDREW: We were in the same office in / Washington.

CLAIRE: For the BBC, the BBC Bureau.

Slide: BBC Reporter, Claire Bolderson.

BBC Producer, Andrew Roy.

ANDREW: Um … and, we probably got there … twelve hours after it happened?

CLAIRE: I think you got there sooner. *(ANDREW: Yeah.)* I got there the next day. *(ANDREW: I got –)* And you had a lot of delays, getting there, it was trouble it was really difficult I remember, I think you called from the plane or something?

ANDREW: There was, um … there were lightning strikes all around the field, uh the airfield in Oklahoma City. I remember being at the back of the plane with a Chinese trade delegation and it was so rough everybody was vomiting. And, the, um … pilot … had some amazing American-Indian name like … you know … Straight-Spear, or you know, something like this … and, just, that sort of incredibly calm voice and gets us on the ground.

JENIFER: Because I was anchoring, I was pretty much in the building um until I went about two days later, I mean, just the, the size of, and the scope of the destruction … It was so much bigger in real life than it looked on television.

ANDREW: Um … and … um … uh, the other thing was the smell. Um, you know you could smell, um … that people had died there, and that, that stayed with us for the whole time, especially … um … uh … in coming days because, um, uh … it was hot, it rained … um … but also the other thing was that we started to learn, who was in the building, so there was a, crèche for children. And, hearing about that, was really shocking.

CLAIRE: I'd got there the next day … Andrew and Jeremy had set up, in this carpark and I remember the same thing of, thinking "God you're CLOSE to it." *(ANDREW: Mmm.)*

ANDREW: And I do remember … especially in the evenings, when the building façade was floodlit, um … standing there doing live shots and you got this sort of almost … amphitheatre. A feeling that you were broadcasting against … this sort of tableau. Tableau of destruction.

CLAIRE: It was the children. That was the / really …

ANDREW: Yes, the children of all the employees, um, I, I, I think that's right *(CLAIRE: Mmm.)* um … *(CLAIRE: Mmm.)* and then … on the ground, we weren't doing so much, of; "Who did it?", in the early stages. *(CLAIRE: We were doing rescue, the rescue attempt.)* We … yeah we were doing. Search for survivors.

JENIFER: So I mean at first I wanted to think it was natural, you know, I didn't even want to think human beings had done it, you know? You sure don't wanna think that some kid from New York with a crew cut had done this.

IMAD stands and approaches audience rather modestly.

IMAD: I was a recruiting manager for Furr's Cafeteria. Um one of the people we recruited was a gentleman, Ibrahim Ahmad, his wife and my wife are both Mexican, and they became good friends, I'd been to his *house*, he's been to my *house*.

I think the day of the bombing I was watching the news, and all of a sudden, there is John Doe number one, John Doe number two, um, story of a brown pickup. I mean, the sensation in the media was unbelievable. I was watching the news and saying, "Whoa! They describing me, right? Whoa. But this was Ibrahim Ahmad, who work for me. Ibrahim was leaving to Jordan that day. This neighbor call, ugh, 911, and start describing those two Middle Eastern guys. Of course, um, when something like this happens, panics happens. What are two Middle Eastern guys look like? And, you know, we're very similar in looks, and once you describe a Middle Eastern guy, you pretty much describe a lot of Middle Eastern guys, you know, big nose, curly hair, *(Jokes.)* that's when I had hair. Um, um, and see then, all of a sudden, you know, Ibrahim's house is on TV. People pass by his house, throw beer bottles, trash … it's a small house, very humble. The wife was so scared, that she took her kids, and she came to our house.

I knew that, Ibrahim was leaving to Jordan that day. He went shopping for some, you know, ugh, presents for his family.

Self-proclaimed Middle Eastern experts would come on TV and say, well, um, this has Middle Eastern prints all over it. Um, you know … Muslim terrorists, um … you know. The news constantly hammering the issue, that Ibrahim Ahmad was a suspect and um, there's a bomb making material in his luggage … Um, I'm very close friend to him *(Short pause.)* this is really, to this day is hard for me to say, but … I suspected him. You know? I suspected my own friend … and then all of a sudden this suspicion turned into anger, why would he implicate *me* in all this.

Um, I decided, well, to call the FBI and say, are you looking, who is John Doe number two, am I John Doe number two? They came to my restaurant, interviewed me a couple of times. I remember that night, was a very, very hard night. And of course the "talk shows"; "There is Muslim terrorist cells in Oklahoma," "They teach hate in Oklahoma." This is way before September 11, you have to understand … and this Middle Eastern expert, I use that term very loosely, because those guys probably just had tabbouleh for lunch and all of a sudden they become experts.

Going to work the second day was really hard. You know, I know everybody, everybody knows me. And all of a sudden, this guy that I know very, very well this guy he's been to my *house* – I've been to his *house*, coming down the line with his face extremely frowning. And, um, I greeted him and then, he, you know, with a burst of anger says, "You people have better have not done this," in front of all my employees and in front of all the customers. I don't know what I was … scared? Or saddened that somebody would think I would have anything to do with this? Or my Muslim faith would have to do anything with this. All of a sudden, the story takes a completely different turn. Timothy McVeigh was caught. White guy. All-American white guy. I don't want to say that we were happy, but, I will say we were relieved.

CLAIRE: There was this report that two Muslim guys had been seen, driving away from Oklahoma City *(ANDREW: Yeah.)* looking back on it now I mean it was incredibly irresponsible / reporting.

JENIFER: I think it's unfortunate any time we jump to conclusions and particularly when they affect a group of people. You saw some of the worst and some of the best of live television, you know? There was a lot I was very proud of, what we did on live television.

IMAD: I did not hear any radio station whatsoever, or TV station, saying, "Whoa, we were sorry that we, you know, um, rushed to judgment and we, pinpointed the finger at the Muslims." They have not invited us to, for the memorial services since 1995, um, so maybe on this anniversary? Maybe they will invite us? I doubt it.

Okay. *(Laughs.)* It's a bit confusing because my name is Imad, I-M-A-D, and my title is Imam, I-M-A-M. Um, so, the title is Imam, I-M-A-M. It means literally "the person up front". So, if you see Muslims praying, there would be one Imam in front, leading the prayer.

SCENE 8

CHRIS and AREN sit together; BELLA is quite shy and sits away slightly; upstage and to the side.

CHRIS: I was thirty, so she was ten years younger than me. So, um, I don't know. It just kind of came like a big brother role. Big brother, little sister role, to where I just kind of looked out for her. *(Laughs.)*

AREN: Um, I was born and raised in Oklahoma Ci … Oklahoma, in Mid West City.

CHRIS: And I'm the same. Both my parents were born and raised in Oklahoma, / so . .

AREN: I actually worked at a, um, it was an insurance company *(Slide: Aren Almon-Kok.)* And I um … if you were

25

light on your life insurance. I was the one that decided if you got to keep your policy. That was a nice job.

CHRIS: Um, I'd say every, you know kid or boy, that's you know, firemen, policemen, astronaut kind of deal. *(Slide: Chris Fields.)* I applied for the Fire Department and got on two weeks before I turned twenty-one.

It was just a normal, a normal morning … I mean it was a beautiful day.

AREN: *(Agreeing.)* Mm-hmm.

Got up and uh, got my coffee and went to the station. My station was … The Murrah Building was on fifth Street and my station was on Twenty Second Street. And it rocked our station and rattled the windows. We just uh, jumped in the rig and uh got as close as we could.

Um, a lot of people I don't think connect the dots, but um … Baylee was actually handed me by a police officer named John Avera. He was just in street clothes. I think he was working off duty or something. T-shirt and he kept, he came from around, I don't know where he came from to be honest with you. *(Laughs.)* He just said he had a … Police aren't trained as EMTs or First Responders or whatever so. He was just looking for somebody and He said, he thought he had a critical infant. And we were face to face and um, I said "Here I'll take her." And then uh, that's when you know … Apparently the … I guess that photo was snapped with him handing her to me and then there was a photo snapped of me you know, standing there with her, so.

AREN: Yeah, okay. Um, my day. Um, I got up that morning and got Baylee ready for day care, because I had to go to work. And I dropped her at the day care about 8:00 am.

So I was at work and um, we felt the explosion. And then somebody goes to me, she said "There's an explosion in the Federal Court house." I was like "Oh my gosh." I was thinking "My daughter is like right across the street from there."

(Short pause.) And I got to the front of the building and when I saw it, I, I knew there was no way that she could've made it out. And so I walked around the buildings and my parents and my older sister found me. I was like "I can't find Baylee." And they're like "Well, we'll keep looking."

My mom knew a nurse there who got on the phone to St. Anthony's they said there's a child that sounds like Baylee at St. Anthony's.

So just standing there with my mother and my sister. And Dr. Niebers walks around the corner with the priest. And then we just knew that she was gone. Chris had put her in the ambulance. They had gotten to the hospital and got the other hurt people out and then they realized she was in there, so they just put her in the morgue.

They're like, "You got to call someone to come get her." And I know they were talking about a funeral home now, but at that point I didn't … I was young. I said I wanted to see her first. And so we walked down to the morgue and then we got to the door and I couldn't go in. So my dad went in and identified her. I never saw her until, until ... her um, funeral.

People think that people that are deceased look so peaceful? And it just wasn't like that for me. I didn't, didn't, think she looked peaceful at all, so.

I remember the next day. The newspaper. I opened it, and there was that picture. Chris and Baylee on the front of it. *(Short pause.)* To know that I'd lost a child, but then to have everybody else see her dead too.

CHRIS: You know when I look back and I think "Gosh, it seemed like I walked forever with her, but it was probably not even twenty feet." *(AREN: Mm-hmm.)* Fifteen or twenty feet that I had walked over there. And uh, by the time I got there, they already had two patients put in the back of their ambulance. So, they were … That was when the rescue effort was going pretty hot and heavy. I um, you know, I um, I checked for signs of life which we do, you know. And uh, I didn't find any, but you know, EMSA has different systems. They have what they call a Doppler like a stethoscope, but it's more intense. It's more than just … It can actually pick up really, really faint, you know, if there's any heartbeat, so.

CHRIS tries to keep it together.

Um, and it's, it's a tough moment for me here, but they uh … When I told her I had … I told the … I can't remember her name, but anyway, I uh, I told her I had a critical infant and uh, the ambulance was already full. And so, uh, I was … the reason I was standing there looking at her, holding her, little Baylee, was uh, sorry … I was uh, waiting on the EMSA paramedic to get, to get a blanket out.

Because um … *(CHRIS's voice breaks with emotion.)* we weren't going to, we weren't going to put that baby on the ground, I was … So … So anyway, uh, so once we got the blanket out and we got her uh, I sat down I just uh … I think I just patted her on the back and told her I had to go catch up with my crew and uh … Um, that was really the, really the last encounter I had with any of that, until, uh, until the next day, you know. *(Recovers himself.)* From that point on, everything for me was uh, recovery efforts. Can I, can I step out just for a second?

CHRIS exits. Pause.

AREN: Okay. We've never … I've *never* heard his side of the story …

BELLA: Yeah. We've never / heard …

AREN: As long as we've been friends in twenty years, and that's the first time I've ever / heard his …

BELLA: Never seen him cry like that. He's usually …

AREN: That's why it's hard.

BELLA: He usually keeps it together pretty well. Maybe for us? *(Looks at her mother.)*

Company sing The Cox Family, "I Am Weary Let me Rest."

END OF ACT I

ACT II

Company members sing:

This land is your land, This land is my land
From California to the New York island;
From the red wood forest to the Gulf Stream waters
This land was made for you and me.

When the sun came shining, and I was strolling,
And the wheat fields waving and the dust clouds rolling,
As the fog was lifting a voice was chanting:
This land was made for you and me.

As I went walking I saw a sign there
And on the sign it said "No Trespassing."
But on the other side it didn't say nothing,
That side was made for you and me.

In the shadow of the steeple I saw my people,
By the relief office I seen my people;
As they stood there hungry, I stood there asking
Is this land made for you and me?

(Woody Guthrie, "This Land is Your Land".)

Slide: "The Survivor Tree from the Memorial Garden. Everything was destroyed directly in front of the Murrah Building. There were the remains of an old elm tree standing in the car park, planted sometime in the 1930s. Everyone assumed that the tree was dead. A worker from the State Forestry thought there was a slim chance that the tree could be saved."

MARK addresses the audience directly, picking out individual members to talk to.

MARK: It was just this spindly, ugly looking thing, really, with, with half of it gone. One of the first things that I was debating, not, not to bore you with the science part of it too much, but a tree's food is produced in the leaves. And if you remove fifty percent of the food production, bein' the leaves, that tree becomes risky from not bein' able to recover from that. So, we said, "Okay, do we sacrifice this one branch over here? Uh, or do we, focus on the whole thing?"

I'm what you call an "arborist" and it's my job to look after that tree.

You see, I think that trees have the ability to respond and to react and so I listen to them. And, and I, um, Well I … well. I talk to trees. *(Beat.)* They talk to me! Y'know? If you can visualize what they're trying to communicate to you. And so, I sit there, *(Waits and listens to an imaginary tree. The tree is speaking. He's heard the tree and now knows what to do.)* Let's just not do anything, 'coz it's been through so much, uh, in such a short time … with the bombing.

I was always the kid who was asking the Scout Master, "Hey, how come those trees are over here? Or, how come the water is like this over here?" I love nature and I love trees … and really, ninth grade is when I decided t- to go into forestry.

I can honestly say this, that, uh I used to have a tree care company, and you always hear about accidents in trees about tree care companies, "Oh I've fallen out of a tree and this," and I go, "No, no you didn't fall. The tree *threw* you out, because you, you weren't doin' what was right."

And I've never. Ever. Been thrown out of a tree, y'know? In my whole career.

If you got a piece of glass in your hand you can pull it out and it'll heal over. Sometimes it's better for the tree if it's just a small piece to leave in, then the tree will grow around. See, unlike people, trees don't completely heal over. They close off their wounds; compartmentalize. Keep it separate.

Everybody experiences different tragedies in their life. I lost my mom, I lost my dad, y'know, we all get beyond tragedy. Uh, my neighbor, uh, lost his daughter-in-law in this bombing, um. Uh, the police officer that lived down the road from my house, he couldn't take the images in his head anymore and so he took his own life.

Well when my mom passed away, I was the only one in the room at the time that she went, I, I, I walked outta the hospital and then I-I was just in the middle of nowhere, just standin' near this couple of trees, you know? And those trees were there for a reason. I just felt that … the spirit of, of trees live in me. And, and, and that's what this tree, uh. I guess means to me. It's remembering that we can get beyond tragedy.

On the Survivor Tree, somebody carved a little cross into it and I-and I remember going up to that and seeing the little cross, and feeling … that spiritual connection to that tree; "Of course the science person in me says, "Hey don't do that! *(Laughs.)* Don't … don't cut into the tree!"

Well, in in the wild, Elm can live to a hundred and fifty, maybe two hundred years old. We're guessing it's anywhere from seventy-five to maybe a hundred years old. And so we're – we're hoping that it'll be around for another fifty years. Maybe?

The sound of radio distortion. TIMOTHY MCVEIGH is barely visible on stage – his face cannot be seen at all. However a distorted close up of his face is projected via live-feed.

TIMOTHY MCVEIGH: *(Low voice, close to a microphone.)* Sitting down here now, and let me make *clear* I'm not sitting here trying to influence you

Am I pure evil? Am I the face of terror? Sitting here in front of you. Am I able to talk to you man to man? *(The distortion gets louder.)* Sitting here in front of you. Am I able to talk to you man to man?

(Distortion continues as MCVEIGH fades away.)

SCENE 2

AREN, CHRIS and BELLA sit as in Act 1.

CHRIS: That's how I got woke up back at the fire station. Our chief dispatcher asked me. He said "Chris did you carry a baby out of the building?" I said "No." I said, I said, "A gentleman handed me a baby." He said he got a picture faxed to him and they wanted somebody to, identify the fire fighter in the photo. Well here was a five on the helmet of this firefighter; that's my number. I didn't think anything about it. Next morning; the guys were carrying in like, you know, our local newspaper, and the USA Today / and then there were newspapers all over the world

BELLA: Can I say something about the picture? *(Slide: Bella Kok.)* The picture is in our textbooks, our Oklahoma City textbooks. So, it's always been basically unavoidable . .

CHRIS: Yeah.

BELLA: Yeah. In seventh grade, you … It's mandatory to learn about the Oklahoma City bombing. It's just … Well that's my dead sister. I mean you don't really … you want to see the pictures of her *smiling*. Do you want to see the pictures of her dead body?

AREN: I wish that the photo had never been taken. And I'm sure that Chris feels the same / as me.

CHRIS: Yeah.

AREN: Coz that made it hard. I mean people would put it on the front of t-shirts and coffee mugs and I mean there was nothing I could do about it.

CHRIS: Yeah, we tried to get it stopped and we couldn't. We tried, we got lawyers and tried to get it stopped.

CHRIS: Friends of mine that I went to high school with that I hadn't seen in years. They'd say "Yeah, I got a daughter and son. My son's name, my daughter is Baylee." They said "We named her after the you know." / So, I mean, yeah.

AREN: Yeah, people would come up to me at like the mall … and they're like "Oh this is my Baylee, do you want to hold her." And I'm like "No. I don't want to hold / her."

CHRIS: When it first happened, they had that fence up around the site and people were planning their vacations to come off the I-40, to go look at the fence I used to think. . I would sit home and go "Oh my God get a / life."

BELLA: People want to have their part in healing of Oklahoma / City.

CHRIS: It kind of hit home why people did what they did / so it's …

BELLA: Just wanted to feel like they helped.

CHRIS: *(Agrees.)* I think it's good.

AREN: Yeah.

CHRIS: Local reporter called me and I guess she had already talked to Aren, because she asked me if I would be willing to meet um, Baylee's mother. And I was like, I was real apprehensive and uh and she … she goes "Well I talked to her and she wants to meet / you all."

AREN: Yeah, I mean she just called me and was like "Would you want to meet him?" and I was like "Yeah, definitely." I was grateful for the fact that Baylee didn't just get laid down, on the sidewalk. Coz I know that … I've heard stories that, a lot of the children that were dying … if they knew they couldn't do anything to save them, they just laid them down to die. And I was grateful that somebody cared enough to not just lay her down.

CHRIS: Like I say, I always felt like I … I mean, I don't know. I dealt with a lot of stuff. Because I felt guilty, that I was the last person to hold her, hold her baby, so. So, that's why I feel like … I guess if I'm ninety-nine and she needs me for something, I'll be there so.

AREN: I mean a lot of the parents that lost kids in the federal building hated me, because their children didn't get attention. I was like "You know what, I would give you that attention if … if I could." You know? It was / awful.

CHRIS: I, I struggled with it. I didn't like being singled / out.

AREN: They would say you know, Baylee is never going to be forgotten, but our kids are. And I was like "You know what? If Baylee wouldn't have died the way she did, you would never heard another word from me." I wouldn't have went out to seek … which some people did. And I mean it, I wouldn't have wanted to be on TV and I wouldn't have like hated on somebody, because their kid was on the front of a magazine.

AREN responds as if being asked a new question about Timothy McVeigh.

I was glad that they executed Timothy McVeigh and I did go to the closed circuit of it. I mean and it's not like I was like "Yes he's dead!" But I never wanted to turn on my television set and see him explain why he did what he did.

CHRIS: I mean I'm "old school". In this Country you have the right to have your stupid opinion, you know? And then you want to … do what he did? He got what he deserved in my … actually, *actually* he didn't; he died way too easy. And I'll say this. Let's say that the federal government purposely raided Waco. I can hate the federal government, but I'm not going go blow up a building and kill innocent people.

BELLA: I've had … I went to a sleepover when I was in seventh grade. And the mom of the daughter told me that the reason my sister had died, was because our federal government went in and blew up the building and killed all those people [in Waco].

AREN: My preacher, he's like "You know the worst place you can get judged is at church," so. *(Laughing.)* We did go a whole bunch for years … I think we were just looking for answers sometimes and there's just not.

CHRIS: It's been a tough road, So I almost lost my wife and my kids but everything's *(Laughs.)* … I finally you know, dropped the *John Wayne* persona we all firemen like to carry and uh, you know, went and got some help. I went to a place out in California. Um, I'll give them a little plug. It's "West Coast Post Traumatic Retreat" and it's all, it's all first responders.

I'll have thirty years in July and I'll retire with thirty-two years on the job. I'll have to stay busy. I can't, I, I don't like to sit around so. Yeah, this last two hours have been killing me, just sitting here. *(Laughing.)*

AREN: And I mean it's hard. This year she would've turned twenty-one. She died the day after her first birthday. So that's tough.

BELLA: It will forever impact me, my kids, their kids, because they'll see their family member dead just like I did …

AREN: That photo; that wasn't who Baylee was. She wasn't the baby in the fireman's arms. She was my child.

The loud sound of radio distortion and a grainy image of the famous firefighter with baby Baylee appears and then quickly disappears.

SCENE 3

REBECCA and CHRISTY address the audience directly, but they don't acknowledge the presence of each other.

REBECCA: To me, it was … it's like knowing your eyes are blue. It was just like that. I knew. I always knew. I was in the / bombing.

CHRISTY: I think from my parents telling me stories, I think I've pieced together sort of pseudo memories, you know? My dad was trying to get past the barricades because, you know, he–he just assumed I was trapped under some rubble or something. *(Slide: Christy Smith.)* They wouldn't let him through, but he was noticing that anyone who had on gloves was getting through, policeman, fire people and so he found a dirty glove on the ground and put one hand in his pocket, and was just allowed through and started digging through the rubble … he found, um, found the place where I had been and he found my baby blankets.

REBECCA: Well, from what I was told, um, my uh … *(Slide: Rebecca Denny.)* Brandon and I were at the daycare center we were uh … sitting all around a table playing with I think … I think it was play dough or something. But uh … and then the children that weren't at that table. They, they all died.

CHRISTY: I was in the infant nursery at the YWCA, across the street. And. Um, as far as I know, all of the kids in the nursery were pretty much fine.

REBECCA: Whole left side of my body burned and broke my collarbone. My left elbow and I had a piece of crowbar, stuck in my upper thigh. I was in the hospital for about ten days.

CHRISTY: I had a piece of glass in my toe. *(Beat.)* It's fine *now* by the way. *(Laughs.)*

REBECCA: When I look at pictures of myself um, you know from interviews or different people just wanting to come over and meet me … it … I just … I have this … blank look kind of a polite smile … Um, and that's just how my childhood was it … I just always had to you know, say certain things.

CHRISTY: I mean, it was never really discussed completely. They said somewhere that they had a box of stuff if I was ever interested.

REBECCA: I think that my, after it first happened my dad really liked to be able to talk to people and tell people his own story, and he loves giving his opinion on everything.

CHRISTY: I always sorta felt like my dad would tell people that I was in the bombing.

REBECCA: He'd take every opportunity he could to make sure people knew that our family was good, or what we were / up to.

CHRISTY: Almost like I had been a, ya know, first place winner in a spelling bee, um, and sort of bragging, ya know, that his child was so special. And, I always felt like he told people before I was / ready.

REBECCA: We go out to restaurants and he would just bring it up with our server for some reason he would think they would want to know, he would say; *(Putting on a "Dad" voice.)* "The reason my children might look *familiar* to you *is* … " because of blah blah blah. *(Embarrassed.)* And we'd just smile at the server and say, "Okay."

CHRISTY: I mean, certainly it impacted my life and my personal narrative …

REBECCA: Well, I used to … I used to let it define me … um … a lot actually. *(Laughs.)* Because in Oklahoma we're very open and people assume that they can ask questions … bring up the bombing whenever they want to … I'm okay with it now, but when I was eleven or twelve years old I should have been concentrating on playing outside or going to a movie with my friends.

A thing that I've struggled with in high school, I was to the point where if I did anything wrong, um … getting an F on a test or whatever I did, I would think; "If the people that survived were here they would have done better than me. I'm not doing good enough" … I don't … I don't feel that way anymore um, It happens all over the world … somebody's getting hurt and we don't realize it. It's not my burden. Like, it's everybody's burden.

CHRISTY: Occasionally the response that I get after people hear that I'm in the bombing is, "Oh, you must be so glad that Timothy McVeigh was executed?" "No, I'm actually not." I am vehemently anti-death penalty. Oklahoma is so conservative.

REBECCA: I just got so tired of people being so angry … every time somebody would talk about McVeigh … which is understandable. They would get angry and I just got so tired of it and I just didn't want to be angry.

CHRISTY: Timothy McVeigh didn't have anything against me personally. It wasn't – the pur – the purpose wasn't to kill an individual person.

REBECCA: I mean … he's not a good person but I don't want to spend the rest of my life being angry about something that I couldn't control.

CHRISTY: I just got back from spending most of a semester at University College Cork in Ireland, which was utterly amazing, I want to go to Michigan. Michigan has this, um, dual Ph.D. in history, in women's studies and history and it's just so cool.

REBECCA: My fiancé … I kind of warned him before … you know … he met my dad … that I was like, "Listen, I usually don't talk about this a lot and I need you to know what happened" … He met my Dad then … we met at Olive Garden and my Dad? Like five seconds after meeting him? He started, and it just went downhill from / there …

CHRISTY: Well, I tell people, to make people laugh, I always tell people I major in women's studies so I have an excuse to sit around and talk about lesbians all day. Um, which is partly true actually.

REBECCA: He knew of it but he didn't know like, specifics because at this point that was like my first time; I had new friends and I didn't want to be; *"That girl."* I wanted to be a … another person … no, not another person. But a *new* version, of me I guess.

Members of the Company sing, Glen Campbell, "Gentle on My Mind".

SCENE 4

CLAIRE: Well my *accent*, well I sounded like Emma Thompson, the actress? And her films were very popular at the time. So when I rang up and said, "Can I come and see you, can I come interview you?" They kind of imagined crinoline skirts and, you know … Masterpiece Theatre. And, that's how I got to be, the only journalist, at the time, and possibly to this day who went to the survivalist, network; because I rang up and said *(In a BBC/ posh accent.)* "Hello, I'm part of the BBC, I'd love to come and talk to you!" And, to them it was exotic and different. And I couldn't *possibly* be a threat. Um, and there was a lot of access, through that. I admit that I played it up a little bit, with the / very BBC accent.

JENIFER: To understand what happened in Oklahoma City it is critical to be aware of other things that happened in this Country prior to that. There were a lot of people who were really angry with the United States Government.

CLAIRE: It had really grown in the Clinton years. There was this sense, that, he was going to give the country to the United Nations, or that, everything was, everything was going wrong.

JENIFER: There was a movement in America at that time, we called it the Patriot movement or the militia / movement.

CLAIRE: It was all bad, and, you had to be *prepared*, it was always this thing of you had to be prepared, you had to be sort of, survivalist and ready.

JENIFER: People were particularly angered over two incidents; Ruby Ridge, Idaho where a man's wife and son were shot by federal agents; trying to serve a fairly minor warrant. Then a horrible incident in Waco, where from start to finish there was this botched attempt to go into this sort of apocalyptic religious group and try to collect what might have been illegal weapons, but there was not even any certainty they were in there. There was a raid *(Beat.)* there was a shootout *(Beat.)* agents died, people inside died and in the end when the FBI went in a fire broke out. Seventy-six people died and America just watched in horror as this all unfolded on live television.

The sound of radio distortion. TIMOTHY MCVEIGH is barely visible on stage – his face cannot be seen at all. However a distorted close up of his face is projected via live-feed.

TIMOTHY MCVEIGH: Uh, you hold it back, it's one of the things that the guy learns, is how to hold back tears. Don't let it be shown. I'm not conning anybody, I'm just being me. They treat me like a trophy, like they got me and they're gonna kill me. "We won." They didn't [win]. In the crudest of terms: One hundred and sixty-eight to one.

(Distortion continues as MCVEIGH fades away.)

SCENE 5

BUD sits throughout the scene. STEPHEN is animated, moving through the space as he tells his story. At times they are physically close to each other, but never acknowledge each other's presence. They both address the audience directly.

BUD: *(BUD prides himself on having an "Okie" dialect.)* Julie had, had met a little girl in the eighth grade, a foreign exchange student from Mexico, Julie became fascinated with how quickly the little girl learned English. *(Slide: Bud Welch.)* And she called me up here at my Texaco station and she was just all excited and the question my thirteen year old girl had for me was, "Dad do you think I could learn to speak Spanish as quickly as she learned English?"

The beginning of her sophomore there was a French foreign exchange student and I think she trailed him most of that first week trying to find out how this exchange thing works, she just became fascinated about it.

I'd take her home every afternoon from school, and we'd usually get something to eat, I, I wouldn't eat lunch, I'd, I'd wait until 3:15, 3:30 and eat lunch so I could … eat it with Julie. When she was a little kid; well … she'd get happy meals and, then as time went by those hamburgers started getting bigger. If she had something, that, that she really wanted to do bad she'd call Dad at the Texaco station … but she'd wait 'til rush period to do it! She'd figured out I was much more agreeable, during rush period. And I'd just say yes, you know yes to whatever, so I can take care of my customers, … she said Dad eh, "I wanna go foreign exchange, with, and I wanna go to a Spanish speaking country" …

She left Oklahoma City [for Spain] when she was still fifteen and I reckoned she'd be pretty homesick the first semester so I, I boxed up 'em some food. Oh you know? Some SpaghettiOs, and crap like that that she liked and *(Starts to laugh.)* boxed, I think I spent about, about, fifty dollars on the food and about a hundred and fifty dollars sending it to her … Anyway, she's in Spain with this host family and all kinds of wonderful food is eaten there, and I'm sending "SpaghettiOs"! Anyhow I think Spanish Mom got a bit upset and Julie told me on the phone, … she said "Dad don't, *please* don't send anything else." Anyway … well I missed her so damn much!

When Julie graduated from Marquette, they offered her to come back in the following year as a graduate tutor I thought God it's perfect. We fought about it and she said "I want to go home and work for a while." So she came home and got a job as a Spanish translator for the Social Security administration. In the Murrah Building.

STEPHEN: The Chief Justice of the Supreme Court … called me about 9:00 and said, "Well I guess you know why I'm calling you," and I said, "I have no idea why you're calling me." *(Slide: Stephen Jones.)* He said, "Well, I'll come straight to the point; we have a question to ask you, and the question is if I ask, would you agree to represent someone who will be charged in the Oklahoma City bombing?"

BUD: Julie had, had an appointment with a Mexican man that couldn't speak English. They were returning back to her office, and got about half way through the building when the bomb went off. Had she been back at her office, the, rescue workers said if she'd had two and a half or three seconds longer she'd have been deep enough into the building, to, to have survived.

Lights lower on STEPHEN.

STEPHEN: I sat in the library of my home, never even turned on the lights. I remember there was quite a storm outside, which is typical of Oklahoma in May, and my wife was out that evening and she came in probably about 11:00 and I called out to her. I said um, "Booder!", which is a nickname I had for her, "Would you come in here? I have something to tell you." And I said, "Well, Raider," *another* nickname, I said, "The call that you were afraid would come, has come."

BUD: I let that really bother me for a long time, I was really angry with God because he let it happen … and … I was angry at … at, myself and I was angry with Julie. If she had done what the hell I wanted her to do, stayed at Marquette, she wouldn't have been in, in Oklahoma City.

STEPHEN: My job and role was to be Tim McVeigh's principal defense lawyer and that meant that I had to see that nothing was taken from him, neither his life nor his liberty nor his reputation, except by due process of law under the Constitution.

BUD: And so anyway, when Sister Roseland called I told her, about seeing Bill McVeigh on television … I could see a broken man … and in spite of the fact that at first I didn't even want to have a trial for Tim McVeigh and Terry Nichols, I just wanted them fried. *(Short pause.)* I now needed to tell that man that I truly *cared* how he felt, and didn't blame him for what his son had done and eh … I told that to sister and she said you have got to go meet him. *(Short pause.)* I remember Bill had a doorbell but I didn't ring it. I just kinda knocked softly. We walked into the kitchen and he introduced me to Jennifer, Tim's sister. And we all three sat at the kitchen table. To my right was the wall and there was some, family photos … There was grandkids in Florida and just, dif- … different family members. The largest picture on the wall was kind of, behind my shoulder, and it was of Tim. And I'm glancing at that picture of Tim on the wall and I wasn't looking at it with anger or anything like that, I was looking at it more, inquisitive, more, the question, how could, how could that young man … kill my daughter? And so many other people? And I started feeling self-conscious because I had looked so many times and I, and of course they had both seen me every time I looked, there were sitting right there at the table with me. So finally I caught myself, looking again and felt the need to say something, and I didn't know what the hell to say, I just, I just said, I finally just said – "*God* what a good-looking, what a good looking kid!" Well when I said that, there was, you've heard that silence is deafening? The only thing I could, you could hear in that kitchen was the refrigerator running.

STEPHEN: I've met him. He's Julie Welch's dad. Bud Welch is um … a very um … unique individual and, and um … he doesn't draw attention to himself. I have heard him speak on one or two occasions. I think. Well, Bud found his way back. From the edge. You know the saying "Once a Catholic, always a Catholic."

BUD: Bill said to me earlier "Bud can you cry?" And I said "Well yeah Bill I can, and I usually do it, quite easily," and eh, he said "Well," he said "I've had a lot to cry about the last eh, three years and he said I just can't cry." And after this long silence then at the kitchen table Bill just looked up at the, at the wall and he said "That's Timmy's … " he didn't say Tim, he said "That's Timmy's high school graduation picture," and when he said it, there was this great big tear that rolled out of his right eye down his cheek, and I could see at that moment, at that moment, this man could cry for his son.

STEPHEN: A comment that one of the psychiatrists made about Mr. McVeigh that he doesn't listen to music, when he listens to the radio, he only listens to talk radio and I said, "What is the significance of that observation here?" And he said, "Well, the *significance* is that music causes you to have emotions, so he's purposefully not exposing himself to emotional stimuli." I thought that was interesting.

BUD: It was all of a sudden like this tremendous weight had been removed from my shoulders. And I think what I found that, that Saturday morning in er, in Western New York was a bigger victim of the Oklahoma City bombings than myself.

STEPHEN: Tim took me through his life, and his beliefs quoted the Declaration of Independence at some length, then went into the details of why he had done what he did, and how he did it. I remember that I listened to him and I was alone with him. In the back of mind I had this mental impression of eh, the victims of the bombing falling through the building as it collapsed.

BUD: I got a letter from Stephen Jones, after eh, McVeigh's trial was completely over, Stephen wrote me a, a very nice letter and he said that ... that he watched me go through my, anguish. And, he told me about his daughter, she was a little bit younger than Julie. I think maybe she was in college.

STEPHEN: Larry King, the talk show host put it best when he asked me "Did you like him?" And I thought that *(Little laugh.)* was a very good question. I um, and I dodged it by saying we had a very good working relationship, but the truth of the matter is, McVeigh was not a fanatic as you might think, he was a very good student. He did have people that liked him and he was a hero, I mean he, he won the bronze star for service. I did not see any overt evidence that 'em, he was psychotic.

In the heartland of the country, from say roughly Indiana, to the Nevada California border and certainly from the Dakota's to the Mexico, red river, that there was a great deal of simmering hostility in this Country, towards the Clintons, eh, ... the two that were really incendiary, in the United States ... if you are a federal law enforcement officer, you can't shoot in broad daylight a fourteen year-old boy, out in the country side in the back, running toward his home, and then kill his mother, as she opens the door while she is holding, a ten-month-old child; I'm talking about Ruby Ridge. And then, when the eh Armageddon occurred at Waco. And Tim McVeigh told me "I'll never forget it," he said "You know when I saw that, and I went there and I saw those Bradley tanks and armored personnel carriers running over American cars," he said "I used to *ride* in a Bradley tank and to think that they were running over, the property of American citizens, that was just more than I could take." In that volatile setting it doesn't take much for a spark, to get ignited. Now, I'm not saying they're wrong, or they're right, I'm just saying that … that's the status.

BUD: My first child died when he was er, er two months old. He was found dead in his crib … and er, that was when I was … I was nineteen years old when that happened and … you never fully get over it, you just, you just don't. I often tell people when I'm speaking that er, when your parents die you go to the hilltop and you bury them. When your children die you bury them in your heart, and it's forever. It never goes away.

Two members of the Company sing:

There's a land beyond the river, That they call the sweet forever
And we only reach that shore by faith's decree
One by one we'll gain the portals, There to dwell with the immortals
When they ring the golden bells for you and me
Don't you hear the bells now ringing
Don't you hear the angels singing
'Tis the glory hallelujah Jubilee
In that far off sweet forever, Just beyond the shining river
When they ring the golden bells for you and me
We shall know no sin or sorrow
In that heaven of tomorrow
When our hearts shall sail beyond the silvery sea
We shall only know the blessing
Of our Father's sweet caressing
When they ring the golden bells for you and me,

When they ring the golden bells for you and me

("When They Ring The Golden Bells", version by Natalie Merchant and Karen Peris.)

SCENE 6

BILL CLINTON: *(Into a microphone and with volume.)* We are more connected than ever before, more able to spread our ideas and beliefs, our anger and fears. As we exercise the right to advocate our views, and as we animate our supporters, we must all assume responsibility for our words and actions before they enter a vast echo chamber and reach those both serious and delirious, connected and unhinged.

JENIFER: You know, my sense of it was that the Patriot Movement kind of started to dissolve because people did not want to be associated with what happened in Oklahoma City.

CLAIRE: It receded yes, partly because those groups came under more scrutiny, after Oklahoma city, um … it, receded / a bit,

JENIFER: And so it wasn't cool anymore.

CLAIRE: Okay, but it's come back with a vengeance now.

JENIFER: Rather than things getting better in America since 1995, it's gotten worse. It's gotten louder it's gotten more angry.

CLAIRE: Some people felt it was a HUGE threat to the United States was that there's a black man in the White House.

JENIFER: There are some lessons that we've not learned so well, and that is the danger of *angry violent* rhetoric. That all the talk, all the game playing the militia movement, in the woods with their faces painted green, preparing for a war against the government. And it might have seemed like it was never going to add up to anything and no one would ever take it seriously, but in the end … somebody did, some guys did; "This is a real war and we're going to make a real bomb and we're going to blow up a real building full of people and if we kill some children? That's okay. We're so right and everyone else is so wrong that whatever means we employ that's okay."

States like um Oklahoma? We're a frontier state. We don't want anyone to tell us what to do. We don't trust authority. We're only a couple generations off the prairie here. You know, I mean, my great-grandmother came in a covered wagon and that's not, you know, that's not unusual here. They're self-reliant and they feel like the government, is getting too big? At some point we may have to defend ourselves … from our government.

Pause.

(To Playwright offstage.) So, I mean I can tell you what I *really* think but I don't want it to be in your play. I'll put it that way. Okay? *(Affirmative answer.)* Okay. Right, well the problem / is this

DONALD TRUMP: *(Through a megaphone, loudly.)* Shall I read you the statement?! Shall I tell you what I'm gonna do? *(The crowd scream "Yes"', "Yes".)* Shall I read you the statement?! *(The crowd scream "Yes".)* Shall I read you the statement?

Wild cheering. It fades. Pause. Light close on JENIFER.

JENIFER: *(Expressively and with pace.)* Generally … they looked very weathered and worn and tired because it was a very tough life and when you came out here and you might spend a year or two years living basically in a hole in the ground. These were very, very, strong women, and they were *stern* and they were *hardworking* and they were no-nonsense and they were, uh, they were generally quite *devout* and they knew *everything*, you know? They knew *everything*. They could *do* everything, they could do little bitty needlework, they could milk *cow*, you know, they would go out and help their husbands build fence. To me, the *American Pioneer Woman* is one of the most *extraordinary* human beings, ever.

My great-grandmother. Her name was Sophie and she was widowed young. Raised four children as a washer-woman, which was the most hated chore on the prairie because it involved so much physical work; *boiling* the clothes, *stirring* the clothes, *wringing* the clothes. My grandmother would say they would wring clothes until they cried at night because there arms hurt so bad. Because she and her kids took in other people's laundry and that's how they survived. She raised all four and got them all through school and I still have her box that had all the report cards in it because she was so proud of the fact. It was a tough, tough life. And there was no government help. I don't think she would have taken it if there had been any; in fact she probably donated, you know?

SCENE 7

Snap to busy restaurant; the kind that might serve the "OMG" Burger. FLORENCE addresses her interviewer, who although unseen is her dinner companion. FLORENCE is flamboyant and in her early eighties.

FLORENCE: My dad was raised, born in Texas … And he was one of ten children. *(Slide: Florence Rogers.)* My mother was born in Oklahoma and she was one of ten children and when I was about eight, uh, they bought this little eighty acre farm. And, uh, I didn't, I didn't have very many dates back in high school because we lived out in the country on dirt roads. No telephone and, uh …

A SERVER enters and presents the wine. He is very friendly and helpful.

SERVER: Let you both see it to make sure you like it.

FLORENCE: My dad, my dad made wine when I was a kid. *(SERVER: Oh, wow.)* I had purple toenails every summer. *(SERVER: Right? From the grape smashing. I know how that goes. Yeah. That always looked like fun.)* You know all the Baptists would come out from town to buy wine; and this was during prohibition days. And my mother she'd say, "Lee! If one of them Baptists is down there wanting some wine in the dark there's gonna be some trouble." And she nagged and nagged and nagged until he let the grapes go wild and the blueberries and dewberries they went *(SERVER: Oh yeh.)* wild. *(SERVER: Oh ya.)* They went wild. So, he quit.

SERVER: He quit?! Oh no! *(Beat.)* Do you want any appetizer or anything while we're settling in?

FLORENCE: I'm gonna take that "O" burger *(SERVER: Ah the "O-M-G" Burger? Ooh, you're gonna love that. Very very good, how do you like it prepared?)* Oh, what are my options? Medium well.

SERVER: Oh Medium well's good. It comes with a garnishment of Kettle chips

SERVER: As I say, the burger will fill you up, trust me. *(FLORENCE: Okay, ya.)* The only way we can bring it out is actually to have a steak knife all the way through it. *(Florence: Okay.)* It's phenomenal. That's one of my favorite items. *(To interviewer.)* Sir you good? Lamb stack? Alright? Okay we'll get it going then.

FLORENCE: *(To interviewer.)* Cheers! Thankyou.

When I graduated, uh, I came to Oklahoma City to start my life. And, um, I ended up going to work for the telephone company, which was – if you got a job with the Telephone Company? Great, you were … as I like to say, "You were walking tall."

About 1965 or '66, I decided that the … the youngest one of my sons was going to take expensive braces. I hadn't worked, I just been "stayed at home mom". And I decided he needed braces, and I had to quit selling Avon and get a real job.

Uh, so I, uh, I started work. They hired me sight unseen as the manager of a tiny little credit union that was located in a hospital.

SERVER: Here we go … *(FLORENCE: Oh my gosh!)* I told you. That's why it's called "OMG"; it makes you say it. There you are, why don't you dig in and enjoy?

FLORENCE: Oh my gosh. I used to feed a family of four on this much food! *(Laughs.)*

Enter POLLY. POLLY wears a small silk scarf tied around her neck. POLLY may stand or sit during the scene.

POLLY: That day started, um, as the entrance of the Museum says: "It was a day like any other day." *(Slide: Polly Nichols.)* I was at the Oklahoma Foundation for Excellence where I was the executive director and we were energetically getting ready for these academic awards – we honor public high school seniors and public education in Oklahoma.

FLORENCE: Well I ended up manager of the much bigger Credit Union. That day I had typed up an agenda and told all the girls that uh, we would have a meeting at eight o'clock on that morning. So I told the newest little girl we had, that had been there only eight days to print me ten copies of the agenda, and uh, she said "Oh Miss Rogers," she was still new enough that she called me Miss Rogers. Everybody else, it was just Florence. And she said "Oh, Miss Rogers, I'm sorry. The printer's not working this morning," and I said "Claudette, uh, round up everybody and we'll just have the meeting in my office; I'll read the agenda off the computer / screen."

POLLY: We were getting ready for that and I was standing, um, in front of my co-workers' desk, um, and I had in my hands the only copy of the program that needed to go to the / printer –

FLORENCE: So, we, they gathered around. And I turn around to the back, *(She turns round acting what happened.)* and read an item off the computer screen, and then I'd turn around and we'd discuss it. I mean I could reach out and touch two of those girls that were sitting at the front of my desk. And at nine o' two, wham. *(Short pause.)* They disappeared. *(Short pause.)* All eight of 'em in my office. Just gone. And uh, I was the, only one that survived out of that room.

POLLY: I'm always asked, "What it did sound like?" I've absolutely no memory of the sound. What I remember is how quiet it was and how all of a sudden darker, and dusty, and rubble that just suddenly appeared on the floor. And then, I discovered that, um, something was wrong with me and I, and I could hear this … I could hear, it sounded like a broken gas pipe, um, and I didn't know what that was and I finally figured out. That was me. *(Laughs and touches her throat.)*

FLORENCE: Eventually I climbed out on the ledge underneath the windows and two of the GSA employees who knew me – said "Okay Florence we gotta get you outta here." I could hear the sirens on the way and the helicopters.

POLLY: *(Touching her neck.)* A shard of glass … in my neck, the artery in my neck. I made it down one flight of stairs, always been very proud of that, and on the second floor, one very tall guy picked me up and carried me down the stairs. It feels like a series of miracles. I, I, um, ended up at St. Anthony's hospital and, uh, um, went directly to sur-surgery, and we think that perhaps I might have been the first person in surgery after the bombing.

FLORENCE: Those eighteen that I lost had worked for me for, in total, a hundred and twenty-eight years. Some of them had been there decades and were, were like family, you know.

POLLY: I was on the gurney from the ambulance, and they were taking me on an elevator, the elevator opened on the other side, and there was my aunt, my mother's sister. And she said, "I cannot find Del." Del, my cousin, um, worked in the Murrah building, on the fifth floor. Um, she died.

FLORENCE: That newest girl; we really actively recruited her, and eight days later she was dead. Another little girl, one of my tellers, her grandmother in Texas was real, real ill with cancer. And she had given two-week notice. Because she was going to go take care of her grandmother. She died.

POLLY: And that is um, something I'll never get over, um, because we worked across the street, and I didn't know Del very well. We lived different lives, um, *(Short pause.)* we did see one another, um, but we'd never, never gone over to see her in her offices. *(Short pause.)* She had had a hard life, um.

FLORENCE: Grieve? I didn't go to anybody. Well, I went to my son, my sister, my little Chihuahua dog. I was a single woman and, uh, I didn't have that, uh, and I got through it.

POLLY: Now for me, um, I um, I've been able to have a second chance, um, to, to understand that, uh, people and relationships are the most important in life. Yes, that's the most important thing.

FLORENCE: You know, that Larry Nichol's wife *(This is POLLY.)* was a survivor. When she sees me, she hugs me like a lost sister. And she's, uh, "So good to see you." She is very well to do *(POLLY smiles at FLORENCE although FLORENCE is unaware of POLLY's presence. POLLY exits.)* And then this is somebody that's on the society page every Sunday in the newspaper, you know?

You know the story of the geese in flight? *(Waits for answer.)* I used that analogy many times in staff meetings. We are *one* team we are *one* flight. So I got the nickname; Mother Goose. The last thing I did before I retired; one of the girls had a bunch of mallard duck eggs. I had them put an incubator up in my office. The girls never seen eggs hatch. No; *oh my*, it was the most exciting thing. They took turns. They'd go up on weekends to turn the eggs. They'll never forget they saw their first eggs hatch.

SERVER: Are we ready on another round or glass of wine?

FLORENCE: Maybe a little bit later on. I don't want to get all, *(As though she's drunk.)* "Erugh eer ah eh," I think he … I think he's recording this.

SERVER goes ahead and fills FLORENCE's glass anyway. FLORENCE waits, picks up the glass, stands and walks to the audience and takes them in. She speaks directly to the audience now instead of the interviewer.

FLORENCE: *(To the audience.)* I'm just an old romantic at heart, always have been. I gotta have music I'm crazy about music, I love my music. The old forties music; you know the war songs oh they're my absolute favorite. But some of these songs take me back to … it makes me think of those I loved and lost. Yeah "I'll Be Seeing You" is the one. In the morning, I float through I turn on music somewhere; satellite music, I think my country favorite is Glen Campbell. I wasn't crazy about *all* his music but it's *terrible* about his health condition. And I like easy listening stuff I'm not big on modern stuff. I was never a big fan of Rod Stewart but then I discovered … *("I'll be seeing you" by Billie Holliday plays.)* Oh my; I think I stuck him in my purse, *(Starts going through her purse.)* he's in my *car* he's in my *house* he's everywhere.

FLORENCE finds her Rod Stewart CD. The SERVER turns to the audience and begins to mime/lip-sync the lyrics to "I'll be Seeing You" by Billie Holiday. He is joined by the rest of the Company who are also miming. FLORENCE sways, in her own world.

END